VISIT THE *Spa*

Tools to REJUVENATE Your MARRIAGE

DR. CHRISTINA NURSE

VISIT THE SPA
Tools to Rejuvenate Your Marriage

Dr. Christina Nurse
christina.mm.nurse@gmail.com

ISBN 978-1-949826-18-0
Printed in the USA.
All rights reserved

Published by: EAGLES GLOBAL BOOKS | Frisco, Texas
In conjunction with the 2022 Eagles Authors Course
Cover & interior designed by DestinedToPublish.com

Dedication

This book is dedicated to the one whom my soul loves. Khaden, you have my heart for life. I couldn't have prayed for a better spouse. Thank you for helping me to write this book and for participating in the activities with me. I am excited to continue to do life with you as we walk in our purpose together.

Acknowledgments

Thank you to my family, Amanda, Patricia, Jeffrey, and Abby. You have shaped me into the woman that I am today. Khaden Jr., you are Mommy's heart. I adore and love you always. Thank you for being an example of joy and strength. You are my Superhero Angel. Thank you to my church family; your love and support have continued to encourage me as I seek to encourage others. Thank you to the Eagles International Training Institute Authors Course, Marilyn Alexander, and my writing coach, Kara May, for your training and guidance as I wrote this book.

Contents

Introduction

I have been told that marriage is hard, and when I have asked why, people say that you just have to live through it. And in my experience, marriage IS hard; from having six figures worth of debt to having a baby who needs open-heart surgery in the middle of a pandemic to overcoming postpartum depression, I have lived through some of the hard parts of marriage. So I can attest to the fact that life definitely has its challenges. Even though everyone experiences their own unique challenges in marriage, we are grateful because God has given us a guide to help us overcome those challenges through His Word so that we can get to the brighter side of marriage, because marriage IS beautiful.

As my husband, Khaden Virgilio Nurse, Sr., was courting me for marriage, I began to write prayers for him every day in my journal. Throughout our relationship, I have seen how prayer and the application of God's Word has transformed each of us individually and as a couple, and I want to share that gift with you so that you can experience all the beauty that marriage has to offer. I share practical ways for how to thrive in marriage that are rooted in God's Word, and I also share my experiences so that you can be encouraged to overcome your marriage obstacles and truly appreciate marriage for the blessing that it is.

From the beginning, God created Eve to help Adam and recognized that *"…it is not good for … man to be alone"* (Gen 2:18, NIV).

As the body of Christ, we are created to need, to help, and to support one another. The marriage covenant is a deeply intimate connection with a person who you choose to share with emotionally, spiritually, financially, and physically. With this deep level of connection, we can help each other to accomplish what God has created us to do. Consequently, your marriage is bigger than you! Your marriage can be used to develop the talents and gifts that God has given you so that you can further God's Kingdom here on Earth.

In marriage, we marry our best friend and the person we will do life with. We share life's experiences, good and bad. During the good times, we celebrate with our spouse, and during the bad times, we rely on our spouse to help us persevere. Because of this, marriage IS worth fighting for.

Collins' dictionary defines a health spa as a 'kind of hotel where people go to exercise and have special treatments in order to improve their health' (Collins, 2021). If you want to treat acne, you may get a facial. If you have a backache, you may get a massage. Even if everything feels good, and you just want to rejuvenate yourself, you may get a mani-pedi or sit in the sauna. At the spa, you can get different treatments depending on your needs.

With that definition in mind, this book is a spiritual SPA, a place where you can go to exercise your faith in God through prayer and actions about special areas in your union in order to improve or reinvigorate the health of your marriage through SPA (Scripture, Prayer, Action)! The goal of this book is to transform and rejuvenate your marriage so that through your marriage God's glory will shine.

The basis of prayer is rooted in scripture, but prayer must be accompanied by action.

James 2:14-17 (NLT) states,

"14 What good is it, dear brothers and sisters, if you say you have faith but don't show it by your actions? Can that kind of faith save anyone? 15 Suppose you see a brother or sister who has no food or clothing, 16 and you say, 'Good-bye and have a good day; stay warm and eat well'—but then you don't give that person any food or clothing. What good does that do? 17 So, faith by itself isn't enough. Unless it produces good deeds, it is dead and useless."

In this devotional, not only do I provide prayers, but I give action items because according to James 2:17, faith by itself isn't enough; it requires action. It is my prayer that through these scriptures, prayers, and actions you will be able to transform your relationship into one filled with joy and purpose, and that you will be encouraged through Khaden's and my testimony. Each action section has both a personal action that is a reflection for yourself called "I Do" and a collective action called "We Do" that you will do with your husband. The "I Do" action will spur you to personal reflection and change.

While we cannot change our spouse, we have the ability to change our mindset and thoughts. Through the personal reflections, you will be able to reflect on how you can improve yourself for your marriage. On the other hand, the "We Do" section will spur you and your husband to corporate reflection and change. This book is organized by topic, so if you need encouragement in a particular area, please refer to the table of contents to go directly to that particular section of the book. Or you can simply read through the book in order in its entirety. Feel free to read the book with a group of friends and discuss the devotions and actions so that you can hold each other accountable. I recommend reading one devotion a day in order to fully delve into the message and the subsequent actions. Marriage is beautiful, but hard and hard but beautiful, and this book will help you to get through the hard so that you can experience the beautiful!

PART 1

Why Marriage?

CHAPTER 1

My Marriage is a Blessing

Marriage is introduced to us in the Bible when God made Adam a helper named Eve (Gen 2:4-25). In Genesis 2 verse 18, God said, *"It is not good for the man to be alone. I will make a helper suitable for him"* (NIV). From this example of Adam and Eve, we learn that we are created to be in a relationship and to support one another. Marriage is designed so that we can have a deep level of emotional, physical, financial, and spiritual intimacy. When a marriage is thriving, you have someone who can support you and your dreams and help you to realize and actualize your purpose. Therefore, I encourage you to be grateful for the gift of marriage.

Scripture: Ecclesiastes 4: 9-12 (NIV)

9 Two are better than one, because they have a good return for their labor: 10 If either of them falls down, one can help the other up. But pity anyone who falls and has no one to help them up. 11 Also, if two lie down together, they will keep warm. But how can one keep warm alone? 12 Though one may be overpowered, two can defend themselves. A cord of three strands is not quickly broken.

Marriage is a blessing because we have a person who can support us and help us. This is expressed in the analogy of the cord of three strands (Ecclesiastes 4:12) which reminds us that we are stronger together. But why are we stronger together? We are stronger together because two can rely on each other for help. When one person has fallen down, the other person can help the fallen person get up. When one person is sad, the other can provide encouragement. Because of this additional support, two is better than one. And in marriage, we have a husband to support us throughout life. And as we know, life is not always easy, so having someone to help us overcome life's challenges enhances our lives and makes life just a little bit more bearable. On the other hand, having someone to celebrate life's joys makes life that much sweeter. And just having someone to share your day with and share the daily chores of life is something that we must not take for granted. Because of this, we are encouraged and reminded that two is better than one.

It is amazing how many things I outsource to my husband, Khaden. From taking out the trash to fixing appliances around the house to picking up and dropping off our son at daycare, it is truly a blessing to have his support for the everyday things in life. On the other hand, I cook, wash dishes, and take care of our son on the weekend while Khaden works as a pastor. In essence, we each have roles that support each other in everyday life. But what happens when one of us has fallen, or needs extra help? We pick each other up.

When I met my husband, I was struggling to finish my PhD. I had been studying in my PhD program for five years and the completion was nowhere in sight. I would stay up late nights, wake up early mornings, and work on the weekends, but it felt like I was getting nowhere. Khaden was also in school for his Master of Divinity at Gordon-Conwell Theological Seminary, so thankfully he understood that my time was limited. When we did get together, most of our dates were "study dates" where we would just sit together and work! Those were the good ol' days.

As I continued to work toward graduation, a year passed and I had to prepare for my dissertation defense. Now, my dissertation defense was like the final exam I needed to pass in order to get my PhD. I would present my research, and professors and anyone who joined the presentation would get to grill me with questions. Seven years of research would come down to a couple of hours! Needless to say, I was nervous and feverishly preparing. In preparation for my dissertation defense, I spent nights in the computer lab and closed down the medical school library many nights. Khaden really stepped up; he cooked for me and even spent some nights in the computer lab with me to encourage me to continue to work hard. I was so grateful that Khaden was there to give me the extra push and care that I needed in order to make it through. His actions reminded me that two is better than one because we can help each other in our times of need or help push each other to achieve the goals God has given us. After all the hard work and support from my family and Khaden, I had a successful dissertation defense, and I earned my PhD.

Prayer:

Dear Heavenly Father,

Thank you for the gift of marriage. Thank you for giving me a person to help me along life's journey. I pray that you help me to see how I can enhance and help my husband's life, and may I be joyous in doing so. Help my husband and me to see and cherish marriage for the blessing that it is.

In Jesus' name,

Amen.

Action:

I Do: Whenever I get frustrated or upset, it helps me to reflect on how grateful I am for the things that my spouse does to support me and our marriage. And I would like to challenge you to do the same.

Write down what you do to help make your husband's life easier. Write down what your husband does to make your life easier.

_____

_____

_____

_____

We Do: Talk with your husband and show him appreciation for the things he does to make your life easier.

Ask your husband what he believes he does to make your life easier. Afterward, share with your husband the things you do to make his life easier.

_____

_____

_____

_____

Now each of you do those things that your spouse does for you for a day.

Completing this exercise will give you a deeper appreciation for your spouse and reinforce the idea that marriage is a blessing. You can also take it a step further and ask your husband what additional things you can do to enhance or make his life easier.

Once you have completed the exercise with your husband, reflect on the following questions together:

How are two better than one?

_____

_____

_____

What are your dreams? How can you support each other in accomplishing your dreams?

_____

_____

_____

_____

Scripture: Proverbs 27:17 (NIV)

As iron sharpens iron, so one person sharpens another.

As I was growing up, I would watch my dad cook in the kitchen, and every now and again, he would take two knives and rub them together. I didn't understand why he was doing it at the time; I just thought it looked cool and made a fun noise. But now I know that my dad would rub the knives together so that they could become sharper, and when they were sharp, they were able to cut through the food better. In essence, because the knives were sharper, they were able to perform their purpose better. Therefore, the knives were more effective in their purpose after being sharpened by each other.

As Christians, we are not meant to be alone, and we have the body of Christ to help each other and to sharpen one another. And as we sharpen one another, we enhance our gifts so that we can fully walk in the purpose that God has called us to. The relationship between the husband and wife is a special one. Marriage is designed to be an intimate relationship where we can be forthcoming about all of our weaknesses or areas of improvement and have someone there to support us and to sharpen us. However, vulnerability is required for us to be honest and share the areas where we need help, and we must be intentional about creating a safe place for our spouse to be vulnerable with us and share. When we do share our weaknesses, we are encouraged because we can sharpen and enhance one another so that we can live our lives according to God's calling.

I am weak in the area of finances. I can't remember ever creating a budget before I met my husband. If I had money in my checking account, I would spend it. I did not have much in my savings account, and I knew little to nothing about investing. In fact, even now that my husband and I create a budget together, it is still difficult for me to stick to it! I am so grateful to have a husband whose passion is helping people with their finances, and he has definitely helped me with mine. Every month, we sit down and create a budget to show us how much money we have coming in and how much we are spending. This helps us to ensure that we are meeting our financial goals. Khaden has also helped me set up several investment accounts and recommended some excellent books on managing money so that I can learn to be self-sufficient in the area of finances. And yes, even though it's hard for me to stick to a budget, Khaden holds me accountable to help me not overspend.

On the other hand, one of my strengths is organization, and that is an area where my husband needs some help. Sometimes Khaden can double-book appointments, and he is constantly misplacing his keys or headphones or hat. It feels like almost every day I am being asked, "Babe, have you seen my hat?" or, "Babe, have you seen my keys?" As I am writing this, I am laughing because he recently just found his keys buried in our garden after searching for them for three days! In order to help my husband organize his time, we share our calendars with one another, and I have encouraged him to enter every appointment he has in his calendar— from doctor's appointments to meetings with his financial coaching clients. Creating the habit of putting events into the calendar has significantly decreased the number of appointments my husband has missed or double-booked.

Now, when it comes to misplacing things around the house, it is still a work in progress, but we have designated areas for our items in the house; it is just a matter of being consistent in placing the items in the designated areas (haha!). But that's neither here nor there; the point is that we help each other and teach each other in the areas where we are struggling. It is not easy to admit when we are weak, but it is important to admit the areas where you need help so that you can grow and improve. Admitting your weaknesses requires vulnerability, but intimacy grows when we share our weaknesses, and it requires an even deeper level of intimacy for spouses to help each other.

Prayer:

Dear Heavenly Father,

Thank you for the body of Christ to help us when we are weak. Help me to admit the areas where I struggle so that I can get help and improve. May you give me guidance on how to grow. Thank you for my husband and his strengths and weaknesses. Give me a heart and the wisdom to encourage him in his strengths and help him to improve in his weaknesses. May we support each other and sharpen each other so that we can have a marriage that honors you.

In Jesus' name,

Amen.

Action:

I Do: Next to each item check whether it is a strength or an area that needs improvement. Be diligent in seeking out help in order to improve your weaknesses.

Put a star next to the items where your husband helps you to improve.

	Strength	Weakness
Eating healthy		
Exercise		
Finances		
Doing house chores		
Career		
Spirituality/ Spending time with God		
Raising kids		
Communication		
Organization		
Creating a safe place to share thoughts		

We Do: Thank your husband for the areas where he helps you in your weaknesses and show him the chart you filled out in the **I Do** section.

Ask him what he believes his strengths and weaknesses are.

Ask him to name some areas where you currently help him, and other areas where he believes you could help him.

Once you have completed the exercise with your husband, reflect on the following questions together:

In what practical ways do we sharpen each other?

_____

_____

_____

_____

How can we use our **strengths** to help each other achieve our dreams?

_____

_____

_____

_____

Scripture: Proverbs 31:10-12 (NIV)

[10] A wife of noble character who can find? She is worth far more than rubies. [11] Her husband has full confidence in her and lacks nothing of value. [12] She brings him good, not harm all the days of her life.

What is a wife of noble character? A wife of noble character is a woman who has high morals and values. As we continue to read the passage in Proverbs 31, we gain insight into specific qualities that a wife of noble character possesses. They are values that promote love, honesty, kindness, and generosity, to name a few. Furthermore, when we possess these qualities, we bring our husbands good and not harm (Proverbs 31:12). Some ways that we can bring our husband good are to make sure that we have a peaceful home that he enjoys coming to after a long day at work; we can encourage him and work with him so that he can live out the purpose God called him to do. Possessing these characteristics is worth way more than jewels. When we have these qualities, our husband has full confidence in us to support his dreams and to follow our dreams, full confidence in us to raise our kids, full confidence in us to provide a loving home for our family. In essence, a wife with noble character is a blessing to her husband. We are encouraged because we can be a blessing to our husbands. Are you a blessing to your husband?

Proverbs 31 always challenges me to look at myself and how I can improve. However, in marriage, it is so easy to think about what your husband is not doing and how you can change your husband because it is easier to point out faults in others and not focus on our own faults. Needless to say, it is a challenge for me to reflect on my shortcomings and how I can become a better wife. One challenge in particular that I am still struggling with (even though I have made significant improvement) is creating a safe place for my husband to disagree with me. When my husband disagrees with me, I can get defensive and shut down, and I don't provide an environment where he feels comfortable to share his thoughts and feelings.

Because I did not create a space for my husband to share with me, our emotional intimacy was stifled and peace was compromised in my home. I was *not* being a virtuous wife. Once I realized the tension I was creating in my marriage, I became intentional about being positive and open to my husband. It is very helpful for us to use games so that we can have difficult conversations and alleviate the pressure that comes from having those tough conversations. It is still something that I am working on, and the more I create a safe place for my husband to share, the more our intimacy grows and the closer we grow as a couple.

Prayer:

Dear Heavenly Father,

Thank you for your guide for a virtuous woman. Thank you for giving me strength in areas where I am weak. Forgive me when I fall short of having noble character, and please reveal to me where I need to be strengthened so that I can be a blessing to my husband and my family.

In Jesus' name,

Amen.

Action:

I Do: There is always room for improvement. Reflect on the areas of noble character below and write what you are currently doing and how you can improve. Is it in being generous, or making peace, or working hard? Pray about these things and ask God to begin to change your heart.

Value	What I Do	How I Can Improve
Generosity		
Working hard		
Helping those in need		
Gaining wisdom		
Taking care of the household		

We Do: Ask your husband what values of noble character that you possess from the table in the **I Do** section. What are some areas where he thinks you can improve?

_____

_____

_____

_____

Once you have completed the exercise with your husband, reflect on the following question together:

Read Proverbs 31:10-31.

What qualities described in the passage do you believe are the most valuable? Why?

_____

_____

_____

_____

What are some qualities of a husband of noble character?

_____

_____

_____

_____

CHAPTER 2

Giving Love and Having a Heart of Sacrifice in My Marriage

Marriage is about loving and supporting your spouse, and *true* love is sacrificial. True love is placing your spouse's needs above your own. Christ modeled true love for us when He gave up his life on the cross to pay for our sins. A great marriage is one where each spouse prioritizes the needs of the other person above their own, selflessly giving of themselves in order to fully support their spouse. Honestly, it is not easy; it requires fighting our natural instinct to be selfish and focus on what we need. As a result, it is easy to focus on how your husband can change in order to improve your marriage, but how can you change? What can you improve on in order to fully love your husband? I encourage you to be transformed by the renewing of your mind and consider how you can sacrifice in order for your marriage to thrive.

Scripture: 1 Corinthians 13:4-7 (NLT)

[4] *Love is patient and kind. Love is not jealous or boastful or proud* [5] *or rude. It does not demand its own way. It is not irritable, and it keeps no record of being wronged.* [6] *It does not rejoice about injustice but rejoices whenever the truth wins out.* [7] *Love never gives up, never loses faith, is always hopeful, and endures through every circumstance.*

Being married requires a heart of sacrifice; it requires love. First Corinthians 13 says love is kind and patient and keeps no record of wrongs. These aspects of love can be difficult to enact because they go against our human nature. Our human nature is to be selfish and want things to go our way. However, in order to express true love, we must be selfless. This means we must be kind and patient. It means we shouldn't aim to win arguments with our spouse by reminding them what they did wrong. In fact, Dr. Philip McGraw mentions that your aim in a disagreement should be to be understood by your spouse; essentially, the goal is to understand each other's perspectives (Smith, 2018), not to win. When we understand each other's perspectives we are prioritizing the other person by trying to fully comprehend their viewpoint. In order to implement love in our relationship, we have to sacrifice our selfishness for selflessness. We are encouraged because love is hopeful and endures through every circumstance.

Love is an action. It is prioritizing your husband's needs, and it is him prioritizing your needs. My two-year-old son loves to make messes and has a habit of constantly saying, "No!" On top of that, he likes to throw tantrums and cry when he does not get his way. Don't get me wrong, I love spending time with my son, but at times it can be extremely frustrating and overwhelming. Because of this, one way that my husband shows me love is to watch our son and give me time to rest when I need it. I know that there have been times when he has watched our son when he was tired, but he selflessly spends time with our son to allow me to rest. Similarly, when my husband needs a break or needs time to work on his business, I make time for him to get his rest. We know that parenting is not an easy task, but sharing the responsibility, especially during challenging times, can be seen as a simple act of love. A simple act of love goes a long way in cultivating a long-lasting marriage.

Prayer:

Dear Heavenly Father,

Thank you for your love. Help me to show true love to my husband and give me the strength to love him in difficult times. Give me the patience to be kind and not rude or irritable. May your spirit help us to love each other at all times and be selfless with the love you describe in 1 Corinthians 13.

In Jesus' name,

Amen.

Action:

I Do: In what ways can you improve in showing love to your husband based on the definition and actions in 1 Corinthians 13:4-7? Is it being more patient, not being irritable, being hopeful?

_____

_____

_____

_____

We Do: Write down three ways that you can show your husband love this week according to the 1 Corinthians 13 definition of love (patient, kind, never give up...) and be proactive in doing them!

_____

_____

_____

_____

Once you have completed the exercise with your husband, reflect on the following question together:

Read 1 Corinthians 13.

Tell your husband how you intentionally showed love to him this week and ask him how it made him feel.

What are some ways that you can both show love to each other using the definition in 1 Corinthians 13?

_____

_____

_____

_____

Scripture: Ephesians 5:22-27 (NIV)

²² Wives, submit yourselves to your own husbands as you do to the Lord. ²³ For the husband is the head of the wife as Christ is the head of the church, his body, of which he is the Savior. ²⁴ Now as the church submits to Christ, so also wives should submit to their husbands in everything. ²⁵ Husbands, love your wives, just as Christ loved the church and gave himself up for her ²⁶ to make her holy, cleansing her by the washing with water through the word, ²⁷ and to present her to himself as a radiant church, without stain or wrinkle or any other blemish, but holy and blameless.

In today's society, submission is an ugly word. I believe it is an ugly word because when people think of submission, they think of the person who submits as being a doormat and not having a voice. However, Godly submission is believing that God has you covered in things that you don't have full control over. Furthermore, Godly submission to our husbands is believing that where God directs our husbands is where our blessings will be; it is trusting that God is ultimately directing our paths through our husbands. Godly submission is trusting in our husband's vision for what family should be in accordance to where and how God is leading him. We are encouraged to submit to our husband and trust in the vision God has given him. Prior to this verse, Paul says that we should submit ourselves one to another, and when we submit one to another, it means that our opinions matter and our husband hears and values our opinions even if he is the leader in the house. Yes, husbands are supposed to love wives as Christ loved the church, and Christ died for the church. We are encouraged because when our husbands are submitted to Christ, we can trust that they will make the best decisions for our families, and submission to our husbands is a beautiful journey.

I asked my husband, Khaden, what his vision was for our family, and he said that it was to do God's will. Doing God's will, to him, means that we help others in sacrificial ways even when it may not always be to our financial benefit. Khaden's vision for our family is for us to sacrifice for others in order to uplift our community. In essence, his vision is one where our family serves others, and this fact was evident when we first got married.

Our first wedding was an intimate ceremony where Khaden and I only invited our pastors. Immediately after we got married and said, "I do," Khaden and I went to Domino's and bought pizza to serve to the homeless while we were still dressed in our wedding clothes. Yes, I was dressed in my white mermaid wedding dress, and Khaden was dressed in his black tuxedo as we served pizza in Boston Common, a park located in downtown Boston. People asked us what we were doing in the park, and we told them we were celebrating our wedding day. We were celebrating the gift of our union with those whom we were called to serve. Khaden wanted our first act as husband and wife to be an act of service to the community. He was setting the foundation for the vision that he had for our family, and I happily supported him. Submission to your husband means accepting and supporting the vision he has for your family and working with him to accomplish that vision. It is working with your husband to carry out the purpose to which God has called you.

Prayer:

Dear Heavenly Father,

Thank you for my husband as he leads our household. I pray that you give him wisdom, guidance, direction, and a vision for our family. Help me to have a loving heart of submission as I support my husband in implementing his vision for our family. May our marriage be filled with love and purpose as we work together in Godly submission to carry out the plans that You have for our family.

In Jesus' name,

Amen.

Action:

I Do: What are your negative views on submission? How can you change your negative views into positive views?

_____

_____

_____

_____

Do you submit to your husband? If not, why don't you? What would you need to change that?

_____

_____

_____

_____

We Do: Ask your husband what his vision is for the family. Write it down.

_____

_____

_____

_____

Once you have completed the exercise with your husband, reflect on the following question together:

Ask your husband how you can support his vision for the family.

In addition to what your husband says, what are additional ways for you to support or enhance his vision?

_____

_____

_____

_____

Scripture: James 4:6 (NIV)

But he gives us more grace. That is why the Scripture says: "God opposes the proud but shows favor to the humble."

God has given us grace. This means that we are not saved by any actions of our own, but we are saved simply by the grace of God. Because of God's grace, we are able to show grace to others, especially our spouse. We don't deserve salvation because we are sinners, but because of God's lovingkindness, he has given us salvation through His son Jesus. James 4:6 reminds us that God shows favor to those who are humble. Those who are humble recognize that it is only through His grace that we are saved. The opposite of humility is pride. Pride is rooted in selfishness and is an enemy of marriage. In order to have a successful marriage, our pride must die and we must operate in the spirit of humility. When we operate in the spirit of humility, we receive favor from the Lord. We are encouraged because when we operate in humility in our marriage, God shows favor in our marriage.

There is nothing more humbling than saying, "I'm sorry" and admitting that you were wrong. During our first year of marriage, Khaden and I were living in a one-bedroom apartment. Now, living with a person in close proximity can challenge any relationship. From dealing with each person's different levels of organization (or *dis*organization, I should say) to trying to find space to get alone time, the seemingly little things added up over time. I remember that our first disagreement when we moved into our own apartment was over the temperature. I wanted the heat up, and Khaden wanted the heat down. I would turn the heat up, and Khaden would then turn the heat down (thinking back on it, it was very petty how we handled the situation). This constant back and forth led to us arguing over the temperature, a seemingly small thing, but the lack of communication caused it to be a bigger problem than it should have been. Eventually, Khaden and I apologized to each other for being petty, and we compromised on a temperature setting that made us both comfortable.

During our years of living in that small one-bedroom apartment, Khaden and I had to learn about each other: what offended the other, and what caused the other hurt. We had to learn to say, "I'm sorry" and admit when we were wrong quickly in order to get along and live in peace. Being intentional about caring for how your spouse feels leads to a place of humility and vulnerability that will allow you and your spouse to grow closer.

Prayer:

Dear Heavenly Father,

Thank you for your grace, and for giving me the salvation that I do not deserve. Help me to reflect on this grace in order to show grace to my husband. Remove the pride and selfishness from my heart so that I can operate with a spirit of humility and selflessness. May you give my husband and me the strength to love fully and to serve each other with humility. I love and honor you.

In Jesus' name,

Amen.

Action:

I Do: In what ways do you have pride? Write them down. How can you focus on turning that pride into humility?

_____

_____

_____

_____

We Do: Humbly ask your husband how your pride has impacted your marriage.

Today, wash your husband's feet or give him a massage as an act of humility.

Once you have completed the exercise with your husband, reflect on the following questions together:

What are some ways that you both can show humility to one another?

_____

_____

_____

_____

How will increasing humility enhance your marriage?

_____

_____

_____

_____

Scripture: Philippians 2:3-4 (NIV)

³ Do nothing out of selfish ambition or vain conceit. Rather, in humility value others above yourselves, ⁴ not looking to your own interests but each of you to the interests of the others.

The exhortation in Philippians 2:3-4 is easier said than done. To value others above ourselves is contradictory to human nature, which tells us to put ourselves first. Human nature also tells us to look out and protect ourselves first. However, in marriage, putting ourselves first is a recipe for disaster. Marriage requires us to humble ourselves and to think constantly about the needs of our spouse—not looking to our own interest, but to our spouse's interests. It is this type of humility that will allow you to sacrifice and say, "I'm sorry" when you are wrong in order to keep the peace. It is the type of humility that will allow you to postpone your spa day in order to use the money to purchase a gift for your husband to remind him that he is special. It is the type of humility that will allow you to show mercy when you have been wronged by your spouse. Looking to others' interests is not an easy task, but I am so grateful that in Christ Jesus, we are encouraged, because we can do all things in his strength!

I have always been shy when it comes to talking about finances. My parents raised me to believe that finances are personal, and they should not be shared with others. Because of this, we did not talk much about money in my household. However, my parents stressed the importance of saving, investing in a 401(k), and having good credit, but we didn't really discuss money in detail. Because of this, talking about money has always been really hard for me. Now as God would have it, I would marry a man who loves to talk about money and give financial advice. Isn't it funny how my husband's passion is giving financial advice and I can barely even talk about money? And when we became married, our finances became one, so when my husband was sharing information about how he overcame financial struggles, he was sharing information about how WE overcame financial struggles.

In order to help support my husband's business, I put aside my fear of talking about finances, and thought about what would be best for supporting my husband and how we can help others. Therefore, I have created several videos about finances with my husband and we are creating a masterclass to help people with their finances. It has not been easy to step out of my comfort zone; in fact, there were many times when I had an attitude before filming a video because of my discomfort. I just really did not want to discuss my personal finances with the world, and I would pout and try to rush the video just to get it over with. I was trippin' big time, and in the process, I wasn't being supportive of my husband and his dream. I really had to check myself and think about what was best for our family and for others. By sharing how we have achieved success in our finances, we could help a ton of other people. Furthermore, once I thought about my husband's needs and how I could best support him, I realized that it has been a blessing to walk by my husband's side and not only watch his dreams come to fruition, but to be a part of his dreams becoming reality.

Prayer:

Dear Heavenly Father,

Thank you for your love and mercy. Thank you for the ultimate sacrifice that you made by sending your son to die for us on the cross. I pray that you give me the strength that I need in order to consider my husband's needs with a cheerful heart. Give me a heart of humility and not selfishness so that we can have a joyful and thriving marriage. May my husband and

I place each other's needs above our own so that we can accomplish your will here on Earth and your glory will shine through our marriage.

In Jesus' name,

Amen.

Action:

I Do: Write down ways that you can sacrifice and tend to the needs of your husband. When you sacrifice, do something that you may not particularly want to do, but you know your husband will enjoy. Think carefully.

_____

_____

_____

_____

We Do: Circle one thing on the list above and do it for your husband.

Once you have completed the exercise with your husband, reflect on the following questions together:

What are some practical ways that you can place each other's needs above your own?

_____

_____

_____

_____

How can implementing the ideas you mentioned above enhance your marriage?

_____

_____

Scripture: Ephesians 5:20-21 (NIV)

²⁰ *...always giving thanks to God the Father for everything, in the name of our Lord Jesus Christ.* ²¹ *Submit to one another out of reverence for Christ.*

The Greek word for submitting yourselves is *hupotassó* which means *to subordinate, be under obedience, subdue unto, submit self unto* (Strong's Greek 5293, 1890). Submitting or being subordinate to one another requires a heart of humility and sacrifice—sacrificing your needs for someone else's. It is not always easy. Ephesians 5:20 says, "always giving thanks to God the Father for everything..." So even when times are tough, even when we aren't getting along with our spouse, even when we can't see the light at the end of the tunnel, we are to give thanks. When we give thanks, it allows us to have a grateful heart and to be more joyful. When we give thanks, we reflect on the blessings we have in our life which helps us to be open to submission. It helps us to be open to being compliant to our husband's desires, and it helps him to be compliant and open to our desires. Therefore, we are encouraged because giving thanks gives us a heart that allows us to submit ourselves to each other.

I love to cook in order to show love to Khaden, and he appreciates it. He also appreciates when I do laundry and house chores. As you may have already guessed from the previous statements, my husband receives love through actions. Even though I may not always enjoy doing house chores, I choose to do them out of love for my husband; yes, we split the chores around the house because we both work outside the home, but I make sure to put in additional effort to complete my chores. I receive love through words, which do not come easy to my husband. Even though verbal expressions of love do not come naturally to him, he is intentional about sending me text messages, or giving me cards for no special occasion. It is through intentional acts of love that you are selfless and prioritize your spouse's needs.

Prayer:

Dear Heavenly Father,

Thank you for my husband and the life you have given us. Help us to have hearts of sacrifice to put each other's needs ahead of our own and submit to one another. I pray that I can be grateful in everything so that my heart will be transformed. Thank you for the work that you are doing in my family. May we give you all the glory as we seek to have hearts of sacrifice to be more like you.

In Jesus' name,

Amen.

Action:

I Do: Write down the ways you and your husband submit to each other and the things your husband does that you are grateful for.

_____

_____

_____

_____

Write a prayer of thanks for the things your husband does for you.

_____

_____

_____

_____

_____

_____

We Do: Share with your husband the ways in which you believe that you both submit to each other. Ask him in what ways he believes you both submit to one another and write them down.

_____

_____

_____

_____

Once you have completed the exercise with your husband, reflect on the following questions together:

What does submitting unto one another mean to you as a couple?

_____

_____

_____

_____

Reflect together on some additional ways that you can submit to each other and write them down.

_____

_____

_____

_____

PART 2

Purpose-Driven Marriage

CHAPTER 3

Walking in Our Purpose as a Couple

God created each of us for a purpose. We were each given unique gifts that we can use to enhance the body of Christ and to give God glory. In marriage, you and your husband each bring your unique gifts into your covenant with God as you become one. As you submit yourselves to one another in marriage, and as you submit and trust in your husband's vision for your family, you and your husband can help each other to walk together in your own individual purposes which will be developed into your purpose as a couple.

Scripture: John 4:23 and Romans 12:1 (NIV)

John 4:23

Yet a time is coming and has come when the true worshippers will worship the Father in the Spirit and in truth, for they are the kind of worshippers the Father seeks.

Romans 12:1

Therefore, I urge you, brothers and sisters, in view of God's mercy, to offer your bodies as a living sacrifice, holy and pleasing to God—this is your true and proper worship.

God is seeking those who worship Him- this is the purpose for which we are created. Yes, there are different ways to worship God, but in everything we do, we must do it for God's glory. Our marriage must therefore be one that honors God. Do you show your husband respect? Do you show your husband love? Do you show your husband kindness? Do you do everything in your power to keep the peace in your home? One of the ways that we worship God is to become a living sacrifice for Him—this is our true and proper worship (Romans 12:1). This means releasing our own thoughts and desires to be in alignment with God's desires, so that we can accomplish His purpose for us.

When we release our thoughts and desires, and replace them with God's desires, we produce the fruits of the Spirit: love, joy, peace, patience, kindness, goodness, faithfulness, gentleness, and self-control (Galatians 5:22-23). In order to know the Father's voice, and to hear His purpose for our lives, we must watch daily at His gates (Proverbs 8:34-35) by reading His Word and praying. In order to know our purpose, we must know the Father's voice, which means spending time with him in order to discern our call. We are encouraged to offer our bodies to God and to submit to the purpose He has for our lives by spending time with Him and learning His voice.

My husband and I love to dance, and we love to minister in dance. Before moving to Boston, my husband was a part of the dance ministry at his church in New York. Also, I was a part of the dance ministry at my church when I met my husband. One day, a pastor asked me to minister in dance at her church. I agreed, and I thought it would be a great idea if Khaden and I ministered in dance together. When I approached my husband with the idea, he was excited. In order to prepare, we listened to the song together, we watched YouTube videos of liturgical dances, and we practiced dancing together.

Ministering in dance with my husband turned out to be one of my favorite activities that I have done with him. Not only were we doing something that we both loved to do, but we were also worshipping God together in the process, and it was a beautiful experience. In fact, I pray that we have more opportunities to minister in dance. We used our gift of dance to worship God together, and I want to encourage you and your spouse to use your gifts together in order to serve God, for it is a truly beautiful experience.

Prayer:

Dear Heavenly Father,

Thank you for dwelling in us, and for your heart for us. Help us to desire more of your presence so that we can submit to the will that you have for us. I pray that you help me to produce the fruits of the Spirit in my life, especially toward my husband. May I submit my life and my desires to you as my true and proper worship, so that your will may be done. May my marriage be submitted unto you so that you can be glorified.

In Jesus' name,

Amen.

Action:

I Do: Write down the ways that you worship God. How does worshipping God impact your life?

_____

_____

_____

_____

_____

_____

_____

_____

We Do: Think of a worship activity that you and your husband can do together and that you both enjoy. (Is it creating a dance, is it doing Bible study, is it listening to music, is it doing a community service activity together?) When you think of an activity, set a date, write it down, and do that activity with your husband. Worshipping God with your husband is a beautiful gift and creates a deep level of spiritual intimacy to bring you closer.

_____

_____

_____

_____

Once you have completed the exercise with your husband, reflect on the following question together:

In what ways do you think worshipping God together can enhance your marriage and build spiritual intimacy?

_____

_____

_____

_____

Scripture: Ephesians 2:10 (NIV)

For we are God's handiwork, created in Christ Jesus to do good works, which God prepared in advance for us to do.

God has created us for a purpose and to do good works! David became a king that diligently sought God's heart, Moses led the Israelites out of slavery, Daniel overcame the lion's den which caused the king to issue a decree for the whole nation to worship God, the apostles spread the gospel of salvation through Jesus, and Jesus died on the cross to restore our relationship with God. What is your purpose? What good works were you created to do? Even if you do not know your purpose yet, you can start by exploring your gifts and passions because these gifts and passions will be used to do the good works that God has created you to do, and we must be diligent in seeking out the purpose God has for us so that we can achieve it. But we are encouraged because God has already declared our purpose and prepared us to do good works.

As a married woman, you have a partner in life that can help support you as you walk in your purpose. My passion is tutoring mathematics, and in the future, I hope to develop an international tutoring company that provides tutoring services in math for people who may not otherwise have access to tutoring. I also would like to build up my YouTube channel, Normal Stats with Dr. Christina, so that people will have access to free tutoring services. On the other hand, my husband has a passion for finances and loves to host financial workshops and coach people in their finances; he runs a YouTube Channel, Urban Finance, which he uses to help people become great stewards of their finances. But together, my husband and I have a passion for helping people. Our goal as a couple is to get enough monetary resources to help people start their own businesses and be successful.

As my husband is passionate about financial stewardship, and I am passionate about tutoring mathematics, my tutoring business will be one of the first businesses in our passion project. It is important to seek out what God has created you to do and how you and your husband can support each other as you pursue your purpose. We are God's handiwork and He is our creator. Let's seek Him in finding our purpose!

Prayer:

Dear Heavenly Father,

Thank you for giving me life and for creating me for a specific purpose. Thank you for giving me gifts to enable me to accomplish the purpose that you have given me. I pray that each day you continue to reveal the purpose you have created me for. Place people and resources in my life so that I can accomplish the purpose that you have for me. As I pursue my purpose, help my husband and me to support each other as we pursue our purposes together. Let us have the faith to walk boldly and with confidence in the purpose that you have predestined us for.

In Jesus' name,

Amen.

Action:

I Do: The first step to finding your purpose is to figure out your passions and gifts. Write down your passions and gifts. I define a person's passion as that thing you can do all day every day without getting paid (for example, playing music or tutoring math), that brings you joy and energy. On the other hand, your purpose can be to find a solution to a problem that really bothers you (for example, feeding the hungry or providing shelter for the homeless).

_____

_____

_____

_____

We Do: Do you know your husband's passions and gifts? If so, write them below. If not, ask him, then write them below.

_____

_____

_____

_____

Once you have completed the exercise with your husband, reflect on the following questions together:

How do your gifts complement or enhance each other's gifts?

_____

_____

_____

_____

How can you use your gifts to support the vision for the family?

_____

_____

_____

_____

Scripture: James 1:5-6 (NIV)

5 If any of you lacks wisdom, you should ask God, who gives generously to all without finding fault, and it will be given to you. 6 But when you ask, you must believe and not doubt, because the one who doubts is like a wave of the sea, blown and tossed by the wind.

Whether we know our purpose or not, we have the privilege of asking the One who created us to reveal our purpose to us and show us how to implement our purpose. So, when we don't know our purpose, this scripture encourages us to ask God to show us the purpose He has created us for. If we do know our purpose, but can't quite see how it will be accomplished, we can ask God to guide our steps and place resources in our lives to help us. Even if we know our purpose and know how we will accomplish it, we can pray for God to give us the strength and endurance to overcome any obstacle that may come our way that may hinder us from achieving our purpose. James 1:5 states that if we don't know the answer or have the wisdom, we can ask God and He will give us the wisdom. However, when we ask, we must have faith that God will answer; we must have faith that God is omnipotent and can accomplish anything; we must have faith that God will lead us on the path to which He has called us. We must pray with faith, and our purpose and how to accomplish it will be revealed to us. We are encouraged because through faith, God will reveal our purpose.

I prayed to God to find my purpose in life, and as God would have it, I was introduced to the Eagles international Training Institute, where we took a test for spiritual gifts. My most prominent spiritual gift was that of encouragement. I have realized that all my life I have encouraged people, whether it is through dancing, tutoring mathematics, or giving friends advice. Encouragement is definitely my gift. And recently, after much prayer and wrestling, I have accepted the call into ministry. I will use my gift of encouragement to encourage people through the preached word and through lifelong service to others.

As I have said yes to my call to ministry, God has placed people and resources in my life to help guide me along the way. It is no accident that I was at a church where our pastor, Rev. Dr. Gregory George Groover, Sr., has the gift of shepherding others into the ministry. He is an answered prayer to help guide me, his 38th child in the ministry, in my purpose in life.

When Khaden arrived in Boston, he was searching for a church and he came to a popular church in the city. At that point in Khaden's life, he was thinking about a career in politics because he wanted an avenue to empower and uplift our community. At the church, Khaden met Rev. Dr. Gregory George Groover, Sr., and he saw that Pastor Groover was actively helping in the community. With Pastor Groover's guidance, my husband accepted his call into ministry. Seeing a pastor who was active in the community inspired Khaden to walk in his purpose as a pastor. As a result, Khaden uses his gift of pastoring to help people to be the best versions of themselves and to be all God has called them to be. As my husband and I prayed for God to reveal our purpose, he sent people into our lives to give us counsel. So I want to encourage you to ask God to reveal your purpose to you and to place people in your life who will help develop your purpose.

Prayer:

Dear Heavenly Father,

Thank you for being a God who not only hears our prayers but answers them. Thank you for not only creating me for a purpose, but for providing me with a way to accomplish that purpose. I pray that you continue to reveal your purpose for my life and to give me a heart of obedience to walk in the purpose you have called me to accomplish. May you give me the faith to trust in you to guide me to my purpose. Continue to reveal to my husband the purpose for his life and help us to encourage and motivate each other as we walk in our purpose together. May your will, and not our will, be done.

In Jesus' name,

Amen.

Action:

I Do: Continue to pray that God reveals your purpose to you.

Take a spiritual gifts test (there are many that can be found online) and write down your spiritual gifts.

_____

_____

_____

_____

As you pray, write a mission statement for your life. It should be one sentence that describes what you want to accomplish. For example, Martin Luther King Jr.'s mission was to achieve civil rights for all American citizens, Nelson Mandela's mission was to end apartheid, and Moses' mission was to lead the Israelites out of slavery from the Egyptians. What is your mission? (It is ok if your mission changes as your life progresses).

_____

_____

_____

_____

We Do: After talking to your husband about his vision for the family, write a mission statement for your family.

_____

_____

_____

_____

Once you have completed the exercise with your husband, reflect on the following questions together:

What is the plan to accomplish the mission for the family? (Write down actionable steps/short-term goals toward accomplishing the mission.)

_____

_____

_____

_____

_____

_____

_____

What is one thing that you can do this week to take a step toward accomplishing that mission? Write it down and do it!

_____

_____

_____

_____

Scripture: Romans 8:28 (NIV)

And we know that in all things God works for the good of those who love him, who have been called according to His purpose.

It was never promised to us that this Christian life would be an easy path. But Romans 8:28 reassures us that ALL things—not just the good things, but the bad things too—work together for the good of those who love God and who have been called according to His purpose. I can think of no better example of that truth than the story of Joseph. Joseph was sold into slavery by his jealous brothers and eventually thrown in jail for an act that he did not commit (Genesis 37-50). Nevertheless, his journey led him to become the second in command in Egypt, and he saved the entire country from famine. Through the obstacles and the pain, Joseph was faithful to God, and everything worked out to help Joseph live out His purpose. Although we suffer, if we love God, God in His sovereignty is able to make suffering work for our good and His good. We are encouraged because it is a reminder that God is in control of all aspects of our lives, and it will work out for our good because we love Him and we have been called according to His purpose.

On March 5th, 2020, my only son was born. Four days after his birth, he needed heart surgery to repair the hole in his heart and narrow aortic valve. While my son was recovering from his heart surgery, the world went into lockdown because of COVID-19, a deadly virus that killed millions across the world. And in the midst of everything, I fell into postpartum depression. Having a baby with a heart defect in the middle of a pandemic where people were dying was overwhelming for me as a first-time mother, and it was hard for me to find my joy and peace. Fast forward to when my baby boy was a couple of months old. When he looked at me and smiled, I couldn't even force myself to smile back. That's when I knew that I needed help. As I talked to my therapist, she reminded me to be grateful for my blessings; my son's surgery was successful, I was surrounded by love and support from my parents and my husband, and I was able to spend time at home with my baby during my paid maternity leave. Even in the midst of everything, I had a lot to be thankful for, and with counseling and the support of my family, I eventually overcame my depression.

And as I reflected on my blessings and my testimony, I decided to accept my call into the ministry in the middle of the pandemic. Yes, I recently received my license to preach; everything works for the good! Even though my son had heart surgery, the world was shut down during the pandemic, and I had depression, God will use my testimony to encourage others through my ministry because I have been called.

Prayer:

Dear Heavenly Father,

Thank you for the times that we struggle, because we know that in these times, your power shines brightly. I pray that through the tough times, we lean on your strength and we are reminded that ALL things work for the good of those who love you. And we love you, Lord. May we use the lessons we learn from our struggles to enhance our marriage and our lives.

In Jesus' name,

Amen.

Action:

I Do: It is true that hindsight is 20/20. While we are in the struggle, it is hard to think about how the struggle can be used to prepare us for our purpose. With this in mind, write about a time when you struggled. What did you learn? How did going through the struggle benefit you?

_____

_____

_____

_____

We Do: Reflect on an obstacle that you and your husband have had to overcome. Talk about the lessons that you learned from it and how it will help you in the future or how it already has helped you.

Once you have completed the exercise with your husband, reflect on the following questions together:

Do you truly believe all things work for the good of those who love the Lord? If so, why? If you don't, why not?

_____

_____

_____

_____

In the midst of a struggle, how can you encourage each other?

_____

_____

_____

_____

CHAPTER 4

Being an Excellent Financial Steward in My Marriage

One of the most sought-after financial goals is financial freedom. Financial freedom is being in a position where money doesn't impact the way we spend our time; or, in a more tangible sense, it is having enough passive income (money that we don't have to work for) to support our standard of living. One of the best perks of financial freedom is that we are free to live out the purpose that God has called us to, so we must be wise when it comes to managing our finances.

Managing finances is especially important and can be especially challenging in marriage because two people come together with their own ideas about managing money and try to manage their money together. Managing money together in a marriage can be an obstacle. This is seen in the fact that of the marriages that end in divorce, 70% end because of financial reasons (Palmer & Palmer, 2012). In marriage we freely give our hearts, bodies, and minds to the other person to unite as one, but it can be hard to unite as one in our finances. Some people did not grow up in a household where finances were freely discussed, and people have different thoughts and feelings about money. Consequently, it is imperative that we work at being good financial stewards within our marriage. But not only must we be good financial stewards individually, we must be good financial stewards as a couple. This means working with our spouse to achieve shared financial goals.

Scripture: Deuteronomy 8:18 (NIV)

But remember the Lord your God, for it is he who gives you the ability to produce wealth, and so confirms his covenant, which he swore to your ancestors, as it is today.

As Moses speaks to the Israelites in Deuteronomy 8:18, he reminds them that their ability to produce wealth comes from God, and it is not from their own actions. In fact, everything that we have, we get from God. But even as we remember that our ability to produce wealth comes from God, it is important to highlight the fact that we *do* have the ability to produce wealth. Because we are given the ability to produce wealth, it is our responsibility to be good stewards of the wealth we are given and to be financially responsible. Our ability to produce wealth can come from the talents and the opportunities that He has given us. We can use these talents and opportunities to create wealth by producing a product or providing a service in order to serve others. However, when we do get the wealth, we must not let pride get in our way, and we must be humble and remember that God is the one who has given us our riches. So let us thank God because we are encouraged as He gives us the ability to prosper!

God has given my husband and me many talents. In particular, I am grateful that God has gifted me in statistics and tutoring math. As a result, I work as a biostatistician at a pharmaceutical company where I help to design and analyze data from clinical trials to ensure the medicines we make are safe and effective. Working at this job has been very rewarding as we develop medicines to save people's lives. As a side hustle, I also tutor mathematics and consult on statistics projects. My husband is a gifted speaker and financial coach. We are able to use our gifts to provide us with the finances to support our needs as a family.

Khaden has also created a YouTube Channel and a business named Urban Finance in order to help people be great financial stewards as well as generate income for our family. My husband and I love to give financially to the community, to our church, and to our family, and we use our gifts to produce wealth so that we can give back. In this process of using our talents to produce wealth, we have realized that it is our responsibility to tap into the gifts God has given us and to use the wealth given to us from these gifts wisely.

Prayer:

Dear Heavenly Father,

Thank you for the gifts you have given my husband and me and the ability to produce wealth. Help guide us in how to use our gifts to produce wealth, and how to be wise in the decisions we make with the wealth that we build. May we give you all the glory and the honor as we become great financial stewards.

In Jesus' name,

Amen.

Action:

I Do: Write down your gifts and how you are using them (or how you could you use them) to generate revenue.

Gift	How to generate revenue with my gift

We Do: Write down what you see as your husband's gifts. Talk to him about what he thinks his gifts are. Both you and your husband can talk about how you can use your gifts to generate wealth and support each other.

_____

_____

_____

_____

Once you have completed the exercise with your husband, reflect on the following questions together:

When producing wealth, it is important to remember _why_ we are producing wealth. Our _"why"_ is our motivation to continue generating wealth, especially when times are hard.

With this in mind, why do you want to generate wealth? What do you hope to accomplish with your wealth?

_____

_____

_____

_____

Scripture: Mark 10:7-9 (NIV)

⁷ For this reason a man will leave his father and mother and be united to his wife, ⁸ and the two will become one flesh. So they are no longer two, but one flesh. ⁹ Therefore, what God has joined together let no one separate.

Mark 10:7-9 reminds us that in marriage, two become one and are joined together. The verse says that the man leaves his mother and father to join his wife. When we are under the care of our parents, they protect us and provide for us financially. Once we get married, we leave the protection of our mother and father and join with our husband. As we join with our husband, he becomes the one who protects us and provides for us. Because we rely on our husbands for protection and provision, we must be on the same page financially with our spouse because finances help us to accomplish our dreams and the purpose God has placed for us in our lives. It is important for us to be on the same page, so we have to be open about our finances and in agreement on how to accomplish our financial goals, because we are a team; we are one. For example, if we have debt, it is important for us to share how much debt we have with our spouses so that we can have a plan to work together to get out of debt. Although it is important to be united as one with our spouses in all areas of life, it is especially important to be united financially, because financial issues are a leading cause of divorce (Palmer and Palmer, 2012). Remember, we are encouraged because we are a team with our husbands, and we support each other in all aspects of life, including finances, because when we unite, we become one.

In premarital counseling, my husband and I discussed the importance of being one. We are one spiritually, emotionally, physically, and financially. And in our finances, my money is his money and his money is my money. At first, I was extremely hesitant to combine our money into a joint account. Initially, I didn't know his spending habits, he didn't know mine, and besides that, I needed security! I needed to know that I would have enough money to support my needs and my wants; how could I trust someone outside of myself to provide that? But as we talked through my worries under the guidance of my pastors, I learned that the key was being able to communicate openly about our finances and coming together to determine what we want in life. It is especially important to share our worries and concerns with each other so that we can work through it. When we determined what our goals were, then we could work together to create a plan for how we were going to financially support our goals and overcome any obstacles we foresaw. I was encouraged that as husband and wife, we are becoming one, and we are building together; in order to build together, we have to be transparent about our goals and our finances because our finances are used to support and carry out our goals.

Prayer:

Dear Heavenly Father,

Thank you for your love and for joining me with my husband. Help us to be one emotionally, physically, spiritually, and financially. Give us the courage to be open about our finances and to be on the same page in order to support one another to reach our financial goals and our goals in life. Thank you for your vision and provision, and I pray that you give us the wisdom we need to be excellent stewards of our finances as we work together. Thank you and we honor you.

In Jesus' name,

Amen.

Action:

I Do: Write down your top financial goal (Do you want to pay off all your debt in a certain time? Do you want to purchase a home? How much do you want to save and invest?).

_____

_____

_____

_____

We Do: Ask your husband what his top financial goal is and write it down. Share the financial goal you circled above with your husband. Together, write a plan for how to accomplish both of your financial goals. For example, if you want to save to buy a house, you might set a goal to save $200 extra per month for the house.

_____

_____

_____

Once you have completed the exercise with your husband, reflect on the following questions together:

How can working together help you to achieve your financial goals, as opposed to trying to accomplish them individually?

_____

_____

_____

What are some things that could hinder us from achieving our goals? How can we overcome those hurdles together?

_____

_____

_____

_____

Scripture: Luke 14:28-30 (NLT)

[28] But don't begin until you count the cost. For who would begin construction of a building without first calculating the cost to see if there is enough money to finish it? [29] Otherwise, you might complete only the foundation before running out of money, and then everyone would laugh at you. [30]

They would say, "There's the person who started that building and couldn't afford to finish it!"

As a large crowd was following Jesus, he used the analogy in Luke 14:28-30 to challenge them to estimate the cost of being his disciple. What do people need to invest or sacrifice in order to truly be considered a follower of Jesus? Luke 14:28-30 is a very powerful analogy because it speaks to the power of planning and taking the initiative to make choices about how to work toward a goal. In the analogy, the goal is building a building. In order to build, we must first plan; buildings have blueprints! What materials do we need for the building? How much are those materials? Do we have enough money to pay people to build the building? Basically, do we have enough money to finish the building? The same is true with our financial goals, and in order to win with money and be excellent financial stewards, we need a plan!

An essential part of being able to accomplish our financial goals is to create a budget. A budget is a plan for our cash flow. It helps us to see how much money we have coming in, how much money we spend, how much money we can afford to save, and it allows us to build a roadmap to achieve our financial goals. My husband and I sit down every month to create a budget. Creating the budget helps us to be on the same page financially and we are encouraged to prepare wisely so that we can accomplish our goals.

Honestly, I do not like doing the budget. It is so tedious, and quite frankly, very boring. But even though I don't like doing the budget, I realize the importance of taking the time out to plan for our financial future. The budget helps us to see how much money we have coming in so that we can plan out how to allocate our money so that we can achieve our financial goals.

One of Khaden's and my goals was to purchase a house. During the time of planning to purchase a house, we sat down and decided to create a house fund where we would deposit money into it each month straight from our paychecks. Creating the budget helped us to decide how much we needed to save each month in order to purchase our home. Prior to saving for a home, a budget helped us to allocate money to pay off our $120,000 worth of debt. Essentially, the budget helped us to create a plan for how to save the money to accomplish our goal, especially because I can spend a lot of money (takeout food is my weakness!).

Consequently, it was important for us to create the plan to have the money taken straight from our paychecks and deposited right away into our house fund so that I could not see or touch the money. This plan made it easier for us to save up for the down payment for our home, which we purchased in December 2019, right before the birth of Khaden Jr. Now we have the goal of paying off our home in 7 years, and each month we sit down to discuss how much money we can afford to set aside in an investment account that we are using to pay off our home. With our plan, we hope to pay off our home in 2028! So even though I don't like doing the budget, it helps us to create a plan to work toward the successful completion of our goals, and it is so rewarding to see the progress of sticking to the budget and accomplishing our goals.

Prayer:

Dear Heavenly Father,

Thank you for the wealth you have given my husband and me. Give us the wisdom we need to plan out our financial future and the discipline that we need in order to stick to the plan. Place the people and the resources in our lives to help us plan for our financial future. Thank you for your many blessings, and help my husband and me to be a blessing unto others as we create a plan to be excellent financial stewards of the wealth you have given us.

In Jesus' name,

Amen.

Action:

I Do: Rewrite your top financial goal from the previous section. In what ways do you think a budget can help you plan for your financial goals that you listed in the previous section?

Look at your banking statements and go through the money you spent last month. Is there an area where you can cut back in order to save for your financial goal?

_____

_____

_____

_____

We Do: In order to accomplish your financial goals, you need a plan. Fill out the sample budget below with your husband. This will be a stepping-stone to accomplishing your financial goals. I know that creating the budget is not always the most fun thing, so set up a budget date night! Order some food and dessert and enjoy the quality time spent with your husband planning your financial future! Make sure to include a discussion for how you can save for the financial goal that you both circled in the previous section.

© UrbanFinance Budget

Budget Item	Dollar Amount

Income	
Income 1	
Income 2	
Side Hustle 1	
Side Hustle 2	
Side Hustle 3	
Other	
Total	

Expenses	
Home	
Mortgage/rent	
Utilities - Gas / National Grid	
Water	
Cellular telephone	
HOA	
Home improvement	
Home security	
Utilities - Electric / Eversource	
Other	
Total	

Daily Living	
Groceries	
Childcare	
Dry cleaning/laundry	
Dining out	
Housecleaning service	
Dog walker	
Other	
Total	

Transportation	
Gas/fuel	
Insurance	
Repairs	
Car Loan 1	
Car Loan 2	
Public transportation	
Other	
Total	

Entertainment	
Internet	
Subscriptions	
Movies/plays	
Concerts	
Other	
Total	

Health & Lifestyle	
Waxing	
Nails and/or Eyes	
Personal Account 1	
Personal Account 2	
Co-payments/out-of-pocket	
Hair (Beauty salon and/or barbershop)	
Other	
Total	

Vacations	
Plane fare	
Accommodations	
Wedding	
Birthday Gifts	
Rental car	
Other	
Total	

Recreation	
Gym fees	
Sports equipment	
Team dues	
Toys/child gear	
Other	
Total	

Dues	
IRS	
Misc. payments	
Family Fund	
Ministry Expenses	
Religious organizations	
Charity	
Other	
Total	

Personal	
Clothing	
Gifts	
Education	
Books	
Exercise Classes	
Other	
Total	

Financial Obligations	
Emergency Fund/Savings	
401k, Roth IRA 1	
401k, Roth IRA 2	
529 Account	
Income tax (additional)	
Savings	
Other	
Total	

Misc. Payments	
Other	
Total	

Final Expense Calculation	
Total expenses	
Cash short/extra	

Once you have completed the exercise with your husband, reflect on the following question together:

How important is setting a foundation to accomplishing goals?

_____

_____

_____

_____

Do you have a good foundation for accomplishing your financial goals? What can you do to improve your foundation?

_____

_____

_____

_____

Scripture: Proverbs 22:7 (NIV)

The rich rule over the poor, and the borrower is slave to the lender.

To be a slave means that you are working for someone without pay. When we borrow money, we use our hard-earned money to pay back the lender. Our money does not go into our own pockets, it goes into the pockets of the lender. We are working without getting paid ourselves; and therefore, we are a slave to the lender.

Debt is extremely prevalent here in the United States. According to Fay from *Debt.org*, the average American household owed an average of $38,792 in student loan debt in 2020 and an average of $8,398 in credit card debt (2021). The student loan debt crisis was a central topic in the 2020 elections, and I know families who struggle to pay off their car loans and mortgages. We work so hard only to have our money go toward paying off our debt; we don't have the opportunity to fully enjoy the fruits of our labor. Because of this, it is so important for us to pay off our debt so that we can be free—financially free. When our debts are paid, we are free to spend our money how we want, and we are encouraged to have financial freedom in order to invest in the calling that God has placed on our lives.

When my husband and I got married, we had around $120,000 worth of debt together. This debt included school tuition (Khaden was earning his Master of Divinity degree and we were repaying my parents a portion of my student loan from undergraduate school), two car payments, credit card debt, and debt from our wedding. Can you imagine the pressure of having six figures worth of debt and being newly married? We wanted to invest in our vision, but in order to do that, we had to first invest in paying off our debt. So we created a plan, and implementing our plan required sacrifice. We started by breaking down our debt into smaller pieces. First, we paid off the credit card debt, then we worked on paying off the car loans and the student loans.

The year we decided to pay off our car loans was the year of my 30th birthday. Now my birthday is in May, but we decided to pay off our car loans first and save up money for my birthday trip to Thailand, which we took in October. Yes, I waited 5 months before taking my birthday trip because we wanted to prioritize paying off our car loans. And this is one of the many experiences that I had with sacrifice and delayed gratification during the period of time we were paying off our debt. It was not easy, but we knew that we had to do it so that we could build a legacy for our future children, live financially free, and generously give back to our community. When we paid off our debt, it felt as if a huge weight had been lifted off of our shoulders, and we were free! I want to encourage you to build a plan to pay off any debt you may have so that you won't be a slave to the lender, and you can experience true freedom!

Prayer:

Dear Heavenly Father,

Thank you for your wisdom and encouragement. Give us the knowledge we need in order to become or stay debt-free. Help us to invest in our goals and dreams and not the pockets of the lenders. Lord, thank you for giving us the tools and the wisdom for excellent financial stewardship. We pray that you give us the wisdom and the resources to become debt-free and enable us to be blessed financially so that we can be a blessing to others.

In Jesus' name,

Amen.

Action:

I Do: As I mentioned, Khaden and I were able to pay off $120,000 of debt in less than two years. We created a YouTube video about our journey and how we did it. Check out the link below:

https://www.youtube.com/watch?v=Xw8EogkCS9k. For additional tips on how to build wealth, explore our YouTube page, Urban Finance, at www.youtube.com/UrbanFinance.

Write down three strategies you can use to pay off debt.

_____

_____

_____

_____

We Do: A large reason my husband and I were able to stay focused on becoming debt-free was because we knew why we wanted to be debt-free. Our "why" for becoming debt-free was that we wanted to leave a legacy to our family and give to our community. So talk with your husband about your "why." Why is it important for you both to become or stay debt-free? Write it down.

_____

_____

_____

_____

Once you have completed the exercise with your husband, reflect on the following questions together:

What pressure do you/ did you feel while you were in debt?

_____

_____

_____

_____

How can you support and encourage each other while paying off your debt? If you have already paid off your debt, how does it feel to be debt-free?

_____

_____

_____

_____

Scripture: 2 Corinthians 9:6-8 (NLT)

⁶ Remember this—a farmer who plants only a few seeds will get a small crop. But the one who plants generously will get a generous crop. ⁷ You must each decide in your heart how much to give. And don't give reluctantly or in response to pressure. "For God loves a person who gives cheerfully."⁸ And God will generously provide all you need. Then you will always have everything you need and plenty left over to share with others.

As Paul writes to the Corinthians in this verse, he encourages them to give. As Paul encourages them to give, he says do so with a cheerful heart. In essence, we should give because we want to give, *not* because we feel obligated to give. When we feel obligated to give, we may not feel the joy in giving. When we feel pressure to give, our hearts may not feel at peace. Paul further encourages the Corinthians by reminding them that God loves a cheerful giver, and He will provide everything we need (2 Cor 9:7-8). Therefore, we can give cheerfully because God is our ultimate provider, and He ensures that we want for nothing. In fact, God blesses us so much that we have enough to share (2 Cor 9:8). So we are encouraged to give because God gives to us.

Having $120,000 worth of debt as a newly married couple was a difficult journey. It would have been easy for us to say that we would put all of our money toward the debt so that we could pay it off quicker. However, in the midst of paying off our debt, my husband and I continued to faithfully give a portion of our income to the church, and we have truly been blessed for it. We were able to pay off all of our $120,000 worth of debt in the first two years of our marriage, and while paying for our debt and consistently giving to the church, we both received promotions at our jobs which allowed us to get more income and give back even more! God has been so faithful to us in showing us that if we remember that He is the ultimate provider and source of our resources, He will not only provide for us, but He will pour out so much blessing that we have plenty enough to share with others!

Prayer:

Dear Heavenly Father,

Thank you for being Jehovah Jireh, our ultimate provider. Thank you for being faithful to us even though we are not faithful to you. I pray that we are continually reminded that you are the source of life and our resources. In reminding us of this, give us hearts of giving that will allow us to give back to you what you have given to us. Help us to test and approve that by giving to you cheerfully, that you will pour out so much blessing that there will be plenty enough to share! Give us the faith to give, even when we are tempted to not give. And when we receive the blessings after we bring our gifts to you, may you get the glory forever and ever.

In Jesus' name,

Amen.

Action:

I Do: Reflect on a time when you have given cheerfully. How did God bless you as you gave? I find that reflecting on blessings helps us to develop a grateful heart and reminds us that God is faithful, which increases our desire to give back to God!

We Do: Discuss with your husband ways that you both want to give (to church, to charity organizations, to family and friends) and write them down. Look at the budget you created. Have you allocated an amount of money toward giving? If not, discuss and write down a plan to do so and adjust your budget so that you can give!

_____

_____

_____

_____

Once you have completed the exercise with your husband, reflect on the following questions together:

How do you feel when you give?

_____

_____

_____

_____

If you had an unlimited amount of money, where would you want to give your money?

_____

_____

_____

_____

PART 3

Overcoming in My Marriage

CHAPTER 5

Protection for My Marriage

Marriage is a covenant that we make with our husbands before God. It is an agreement that we will live the rest of our lives with our husbands through good and bad times. As such, it is our duty, along with our husbands', to protect our marriages. We must protect the covenant that we made before God because there are many temptations in the world and forces that seek to destroy the vows we have made with our husbands, but the beauty is that God gives us the strength and wisdom that we need to protect our marriages through His Word.

Scripture: Proverbs 21:9 (NLT)

It's better to live alone in the corner of an attic than with a quarrelsome wife in a lovely home.

In Proverbs 21:9, living in a corner of the attic (not even the whole attic) alone is declared better than living in a beautiful home with a woman who stirs up drama. Being in the corner of an attic alone is better than a beautiful home with a wife who is argumentative, because of the peace. Peace is worth coming home to. Peace after a hard day at work is refreshing; peace is worth more than earthly goods. When someone is quarrelsome, it causes strife and stress. An environment with someone who is quarrelsome is not a healthy environment and certainly not an environment that we would like to come home to. We are therefore encouraged to protect our marriage by making every effort to provide a peaceful home.

I remember asking Khaden what is the one thing that he values that he would like for me to give him. My husband's answer was simple: "I want peace." And as I have thought about this, I begin to understand more and more why my husband responded how he did. Peace enables my husband to be calm in a world where he is fighting to provide for our family. He wants peace because it gives him a chance to breathe and regroup after a tough day at work.

Peace gives my husband something to look forward to coming home to. When Khaden said that he wants peace, I became intentional about making sure that our home was a peaceful environment by greeting him with a smile when he came home, asking him how his day was, and making sure that I show him love through cooking him a nice hot meal. Even when we have our disagreements, we are intentional about making sure that we come to a solution by talking it out so that we don't have hostility in our home. When tensions are high, we make an effort to step away until we can talk with a level head. Peace is so valuable to protecting our marriage because it enables us to look forward to and enjoy coming together with our spouses.

Prayer:

Dear Heavenly Father,

Thank you for being Jehovah Shalom, the God of Peace. I pray that you enable my husband and me to have a peaceful home so that we may enjoy being in each other's presence. May we enjoy each other and love one another so that we can protect the covenant that we made before you and be married until death do us part. Lord, we love you and we honor you.

In Jesus' name,

Amen.

Action:

I Do: Write down ways that you can create a peaceful home for you and your husband.

_____

_____

_____

_____

We Do: Circle one of the above ways you can create a peaceful home and do it today! Make a commitment to implement the ways that you have written down to create a peaceful home throughout your lifetime.

Once you have completed the exercise with your husband, reflect on the following questions together:

How important is it to you to have peace in our home?

_____

_____

_____

_____

In what ways is our home not at peace? How can we change that?

_____

_____

_____

_____

_____

If we had peace in the home, how would it impact our marriage?

_____

_____

_____

_____

_____

_____

Scripture: Ephesians 4:2-3 (NIV)

² *Be completely humble and gentle; be patient, bearing with one another in love.* ³ *Make every effort to keep the unity of the Spirit through the bond of peace.*

The words of Ephesians 4:2-3— be completely humble and gentle, be patient—can be especially challenging when your spouse has caused you to be upset. These things are all easy when things are going well. However, it is during the times of hardship that being completely humble, gentle, and patient are especially important. With humility, we can admit when we are wrong; with gentleness, we can show compassion when our spouse is wrong; and with patience and love, we can bring peace into our marriages. Ephesians 4:3 takes it a step further to say, "Make *every* effort to keep the unity of the Spirit through the bond of peace." Make *every* effort to keep unity through peace. Whew, try doing that when your spouse forgets to pick up the kids, or he spent all of your savings without telling you! It is hard! But through God's strength, it is possible. How do we bring peace? Through humility, gentleness, and patience. As we meditate on God's word, we begin to exude these qualities. We can be encouraged when going through hardships because His word is the guide to living a life full of joy, peace, and love.

I used to nag Khaden about leaving crumbs around the house. I mean, I could tell where he ate and what he ate just by looking at the trail of crumbs. It would cause tension between us and honestly, nagging would not solve anything because I would still see the crumbs. I finally had to have a heart to heart with myself. Is nagging my husband about crumbs worth the disruption in peace that it brings? No. Does nagging him about leaving crumbs actually help the situation? No. Does his leaving crumbs outweigh all of the good things that he does for our family? Absolutely not!

With this new mindset, I made the decision to clean up the crumbs in order to keep the peace - without nagging. Something as small as cleaning crumbs peacefully has helped to enhance my marriage. For me, it was a mindset shift. When I put cleaning up the crumbs into perspective with the bigger picture of having a wonderful man who loves me and supports me to the fullest, it was an obvious choice. Yes, it can be annoying, but when I think about all of the good things that my husband does for me, I think it is the least that I can do in order to have a peaceful marriage.

Prayer:

Dear Heavenly Father,

Thank you for your Word that guides us. Thank you for your spirit that guides and binds us as one unit. I pray for peace in my marriage, and I ask you to help my husband and me to rely on your Spirit of peace. Thank you for your spirit that guides and binds us as one unit. I pray that we can rely on your spirit to give us humility and gentleness especially during the times we are wronged. Thank you for your forgiveness. Help me to freely forgive my husband as you freely forgive me.

In Jesus' name,

Amen.

Action:

I Do: What are some ways that you don't keep the peace in your home? Think about ways that you can keep the peace when your spouse upsets you and write them below.

_____

_____

_____

_____

We Do: Talk to your husband and ask him what are some things that you do or can do that can bring peace into your marriage.

Once you have completed the exercise with your husband, reflect on the following questions together:

How do humility, gentleness, and patience lead to peace?

_____

_____

_____

_____

What are some ways you can be more humble and gentle in your marriage?

_____

_____

_____

_____

Scripture: 1 Corinthians 10:13 and James 4:7 (*NIV*)

1 Corinthians 10:13

No temptation has overtaken you except what is common to mankind. And God is faithful; he will not let you be tempted beyond what you can bear. But when you are tempted, he will also provide a way out so that you can endure it.

James 4:7

Submit yourselves, then to God. Resist the devil, and he will flee from you.

We know that we enter into a covenant relationship with God and our spouse when we enter into marriage. Because of this covenant relationship, dark forces seek to destroy the union that God has put together. But there is great news! God doesn't allow us to be tempted more than we can bear, and he also provides us a way out! But we first have to submit to God. When we submit to God, we rely on His strength to help us fight the enemy. We submit to God by not only reading His word, but by being obedient to His word. When we are obedient to His word, we are able to live by the Holy Spirit and produce the fruits of the Spirit, which include love, joy, peace, patience, and self-control (Galatians 5:22-23). It is self-control which will help us to resist temptation.

So when you and your spouse are tempted to be disrespectful to each other, tempted to cheat, tempted to walk out of the marriage, God is faithful and will give us the strength to do what is right according to His will. And we are encouraged to submit to God so that we can resist the enemy and not fall into temptation.

While Khaden and I were in pre-marital counseling, we talked about the importance of having boundaries in our marriage. Boundaries are put in place to help us resist temptation because as we know, temptation is everywhere! One of the boundaries we have in place is that we share our passwords with each other, including social media accounts. By sharing our passwords, we have a higher level of accountability, which allows us to help each other to resist temptation. We also agreed to let each other know when we are going out with people of the opposite sex; for example, when I want to have lunch with a male co-worker of mine, I let my husband know. For us, it is important to be transparent about our interactions with others. Now the boundaries we set may not be the same boundaries you set in your marriage. The important thing is to be transparent and open with your spouse. By being transparent with your spouse, you can make decisions to help protect your marriage from temptation.

Prayer:

Dear Heavenly Father,

Thank you for your love. Thank you for the opportunity to come into your presence Lord. Thank you for giving us the strength to resist temptation. Help my spouse and me to be honest to each other about the temptations we face so that we can hold each other accountable. Let us continue to hear each other's concerns and be receptive to making adjustments that will allow us to protect our marriage. Continue to protect us from temptation and not tempt us more than we can bear. When we are tempted, help us to yield to a way out of the temptation and to rely on your strength and not our own. Lord, help my husband and me to affair-proof our marriage and help us to endure using your strength. Let us keep our minds and hearts on You and the work you will have us to accomplish. We pray for your protection. We love you.

In Jesus' name,

Amen.

Action:

I Do: Are there some areas of your marriage that need to be protected? Write them down. How do you set boundaries to protect them?

_____

_____

_____

_____

We Do: Ask your husband about areas of your marriage that he feels needs to be protected. Discuss with your spouse the boundaries you have set to protect your marriage and write them down.

_____

_____

_____

_____

Once you have completed the exercise with your husband, reflect on the following questions together:

What are some Bible verses that we can use to help us resist temptation?

_____

_____

_____

_____

In what ways can we support each other in resisting temptation?

_____

_____

_____

_____

Scripture: Ecclesiastes 9:9 (NLT)

Live happily with the woman you love through all the meaningless days of life that God has given you under the sun. The wife God gives you is your reward for all your earthly toil.

In Ecclesiastes 9, the author is pouring out the wisdom he has learned about how to live our lives the best way we can. The author consistently uses the word meaningless to describe life. But this definition of meaningless does not mean that life does not have meaning; this term essentially highlights the fact that our time on Earth is temporary and unpredictable (BibleProject, 2016). Because life is too short, we should enjoy our spouses in the midst of everything that goes on in the world. Even as we work and have other priorities, we should take time to prioritize our spouse. Ecclesiastes 9:9 reminds us that we as wives are blessings to our husbands and we are charged to live happily with our spouses.

Though there are times when we aren't getting along with our husbands, remember we are fighting against the forces that seek to destroy our marriages—not each other. And when we take time to prioritize and enjoy time with our spouses, we are investing in our marriages. We are investing in our happiness with our spouses, and we are creating a space where we look forward to spending time with our husbands, which will help us to protect our marriage. So we are encouraged to be proactive in enjoying each other's company in the midst of this uncertain world.

One of the things that Khaden and I love to do is watch movies and anime together. Granted, he loves to watch sci-fi movies and I love to watch comedy, so we definitely have different tastes in movies. But we typically do agree on the anime that we watch. We love watching anime with the underdog stories; I find them to be very encouraging and help to pump me up to take on life. Because we have different tastes in movies, we take turns choosing the movies we enjoy, and even picking movies from totally different genres to explore. Watching movies and anime is one of the ways that we choose to enjoy each other's company and something we look forward to.

We also love to travel and explore new places. In fact, as I am finishing up this book, I am in Jamaica, taking a much-needed vacation with my husband, Khaden. The weather is nice and sunny, the people are friendly, and we finally get to sleep in without our two-year-old son waking us up at 6 am in the morning! One of our goals is to travel to all seven continents and all of the Caribbean Islands. One of my favorite trips was our trip to St. Lucia. We rode around and had a private tour of the island, and we bathed in the Sulphur Springs which is in a volcanic area in St. Lucia. I will never forget the warm muddy water, the smell of the sulfur, and the enjoyment of experiencing something new with my husband. The time we spend together doing things that we enjoy helps us to create beautiful memories and gives us something to look forward to doing together. This keeps us wanting to spend more and more time together.

Prayer:

Dear Heavenly Father,

Thank you for my husband. I pray that we both have a positive outlook on this journey we call life. Help us to rely on you for patience and joy. Lord, I pray that my husband and I can live happily and enjoy our life together as husband and wife, as Ecclesiastes exhorts us to. Help me to place my faith in you and continue to protect our marriage from the forces that seek to destroy it. Give us peace and let your Spirit dwell in our marriage so that we can enjoy our life together.

In Jesus' name,

Amen.

Action:

I Do: Write out activities that you and your husband enjoy doing together.

_____

_____

_____

_____

We Do: Using one or more of the activities above, plan a date night for you and your husband, then do it!

Once you have completed the exercise with your husband, reflect on the following questions together:

How does making happy memories help to protect your marriage?

Together, plan your next date and set a time to do it.

_____

_____

_____

_____

Scripture: Galatians 5:16 (NIV)

So I say, walk by the Spirit and you will not gratify the desires of the flesh.

In Galatians 5:16, Paul tells the churches in Galatia to walk by the Spirit. When we walk by the Spirit, we use the Holy Spirit to guide our thoughts and actions. When we walk by the Spirit, we do not seek to satisfy the desires of our flesh, and we are able to avoid temptation, and avoiding temptation is how we protect our marriage. So _how_ do we walk by the Spirit? It starts by being knowledgeable in God's word. When we know God's word, we learn how to discern the voice of God and how to apply it to our everyday lives. Next, once we know God's voice, we must be obedient to His word and live it out. When we live out God's word, we are able to walk by the Spirit. We are encouraged to walk by the Spirit and live according to God's word so that we are able to deny temptation and not gratify the desires of the flesh.

Because walking by the Spirit requires us to know God's word, I enjoy memorizing scripture so that I can apply it to my life. I find that this is especially helpful in my marriage particularly because I can be impatient and extremely emotional sometimes.

One of my favorite verses that helps me to keep my calm is Proverbs 15:18, "A hot-tempered person stirs up conflict, but the one who is patient calms a quarrel." My son is approaching his, what I like to call, "terrific twos." Because of this he loves to push back and defy me, he whines constantly, and he likes to throw tantrums.

One time, when my husband and I were on a church conference call, my son, KJ, asked for cheese. My husband and I calmly explained that we were not able to get the cheese at that time. KJ stood up, yelled, "No!" threw my phone across the room and then proceeded to yell, "No!" while pushing the lamp down to the floor. Clearly, my son had lost his mind! My husband and I sternly told my son to wait until we were able to get him the cheese, but I almost lost my mind too! How dare KJ throw my phone and tell me no! Thank God that His Spirit lives within me! I was finally able to get my son to calm down and later give him some cheese when I was able to take a break from the conference call.

But Proverbs 15:18 reminds me to be patient so that I can keep the peace in my home which enables me to protect my marriage. It is not easy, especially in the heat of the moment, but the more we memorize scripture and write it on our hearts, the better able we are to deny our fleshly desires.

Prayer:

Dear Heavenly Father,

Thank you for another day to worship you with our actions. Thank you for your love and kindness and forgiveness. Forgive me for those times when I do not walk by the Spirit and I seek to gratify my flesh. Lord, help me to rely on the Spirit. I pray that my husband and I will be led by the Holy Spirit to avoid any temptation that comes our way. Protect us Lord, lead us not into temptation. Help us to lean not on our own understanding, but give us the discernment we need to protect our marriage. Thank you for your guidance. May my husband and I grow closer and keep our eyes, minds, and hearts focused on you.

In Jesus' name,

Amen.

Action:

I Do: The key to walking in the Spirit is to know God's Word. Set aside time each day to read and reflect on God's word, even if it is just 5 minutes. I challenge you to write and memorize at least one Bible verse each month. Write down a memory verse for this month.

_____

_____

_____

_____

_____

_____

We Do: Choose a Bible verse that applies to your life at the moment and memorize the verse with your husband. It can be the same as the verse in the **I Do** section above, or a different verse.

_____

_____

_____

_____

Once you have completed the exercise with your husband, reflect on the following questions together:

In what ways do you think memorizing Bible verses can enhance your marriage? What are some ways we can use to help make memorizing scripture easier?

_____

_____

_____

_____

In what ways do we need to work on not gratifying our flesh? What verses can help us in the areas where we are weak?

_____

_____

_____

_____

CHAPTER 6

Enduring Hard Times in My Marriage

As we seek to accomplish our purpose in life, there will be hard times simply because life is not easy. There are ups and downs, highs and lows, and this is especially true in marriage because two imperfect people are working to build one life together in an imperfect world. Because we are imperfect, we do not always act in love, which hurts our spouse. When we hurt our spouse, forgiveness and mercy are the keys to restoring our marital relationship, which enables us to have a happy and healthy marriage. We can forgive because Christ forgave us. It is in the humility of knowing that we aren't perfect that we can extend mercy to our spouse so that we can keep peace and provide restoration in our marriage.

Because this world is imperfect, there will be many obstacles that we face, internally and externally, that we must overcome in order to accomplish what God has called us to do. Internally, we may face negative thoughts telling us that we can't complete God's mission for our lives. Externally, we may have sicknesses that impact us physically or we may encounter people who simply don't like us or want to see us win. But it is when we are facing those hard times that we as Christians can have peace because we lean on God's strength. God is omnipotent and there is no obstacle that we cannot overcome with Him on our side.

Because Christ has already won the victory, we are encouraged to make it through the hard times so that we can fully enjoy and appreciate our blessings. Enduring through the hard times makes us appreciate the good times even more. And as we work through and get through the hard times in our marriages with our husbands, we experience a deeper level of intimacy in marriage because we are reassured that together with God, we can overcome the challenges of this world so that we can fully live out our purpose.

Scripture: Jeremiah 29:10-11 (NIV)

¹⁰ *This is what the Lord says, "When seventy years are completed for Babylon, I will come to you and fulfill my good promise to bring you back to this place. ¹¹ For I know the plans I have for you," declares the Lord, "plans to prosper you and not to harm you, plans to give you hope and a future."*

In the midst of the Israelites being in exile in Babylon, a strange land—a land that was not their home—Jeremiah declared to the Israelites that God had plans to prosper them and to give them hope. In verse 10, the Lord promises to fulfill his promise after 70 years of the Israelites being in exile. So the Israelites would have to stay in this strange land for 70 years before returning to their home. SEVENTY YEARS! I am sure the Israelites would have loved to be free from exile sooner than 70 years, but that was not God's plan. In the midst of the suffering of the Israelites while being in exile, Jeremiah said these words from God to encourage the Israelites.

Yes, you are in exile; yes, you will be here for 70 years; yes, I can see your suffering, but I have plans for you, and my plans are to give you a hope and a future, God says to the Israelites (Jeremiah 29:11). From this example, we are reminded that God has a plan for us. These words remind us that even in the midst of our suffering, God has a plan for us even when it is not according to our timing. We must remember these words when we are fighting with our spouse or when we are going through the trials of life within our marriages. In the midst of trying times, we must constantly remind ourselves of God's promises. God loves marriage and is the creator of marriage. He wants to prosper us and our marriages. We are encouraged because God plans to give us a hope and a future, even if it is not in our timing.

I was struggling in my PhD program, and I was ready to get out! When I was in graduate school for my PhD, my classmates and I were required to take two years of classes. After the third semester of classes, we were required to pass an exam in order to move forward to the research part of the PhD program. When I took the exam, I failed it, but I had one more opportunity to pass. When I took the exam the second time, thankfully, I passed. Now, I had the opportunity to start my research, but I needed to pass another exam in order to complete my PhD program. The exam I had to take was an oral exam, so I had to create a presentation about my research proposal, present it to a panel of three professors, and then answer the professors' questions about the presentation. Well, I conditionally passed this exam, which meant I had to retake it. (Let me tell you, getting this PhD, was such a journey!)

There were other obstacles that I faced in my program, and instead of graduating in the five-year time frame when most people finish the program, I graduated in seven years. I was ashamed and embarrassed because I was the last of my classmates to graduate. I was struggling! However, it was in those last two years that I met the one whom my soul loved, my husband, Khaden. God had a plan and all things worked out in his timing! My plan was to graduate in five years and move back down south to be closer to home. But I am so glad that God had a better plan! While I was struggling to get out of graduate school, Khaden was so helpful (staying up late nights with me, feeding me) and encouraging and gave me the extra push that I needed in order to successfully complete my PhD program. So in the midst of our struggles or when things don't go our way in the timing that we expect, we can remember that God has a plan for us—a plan to prosper us and give us hope.

Prayer:

Dear Heavenly Father,

Thank you for the times of trial which make us stronger. Help us to remember that in times of trial, you are always with us and we can rely on your strength and your promise to give us hope and a future. Help us to remember that trials produce faith and allow your glory to shine brightly, especially when things don't go according to our timing or our plan. Help us to remember that you have plans to prosper us so that we can endure. Thank you, Lord, for loving us and we pray for peace in the midst of the storm as we hold on to the hope that you give us.

In Jesus' name,

Amen.

Action:

I Do: Reflect on a time when your plan was different from God's plan. Write down how you prospered and how you learned to trust in God's plan.

_____

_____

_____

_____

We Do: What trial have you faced or are you facing with your spouse? Write a declaration of endurance through this trial and God prospering your marriage.

_____

_____

_____

Once you have completed the exercise with your husband, reflect on the following questions together:

What encouragement do you have that difficult times can lead you to be hopeful after reading Jeremiah 29:10-11? What type of future do you hope for?

_____

_____

_____

_____

How can enduring difficult times cause you to feel hopeless?

_____

_____

_____

_____

Scripture: Ecclesiastes 3:1,4 (NIV)

³ _There is a time for everything, and a season for every activity under the heavens._ ⁴ _...a time to weep and a time to laugh, a time to mourn and a time to dance..._

In Ecclesiastes 3, the author describes the different seasons in life. This scripture reinforces the fact that it is inevitable that life will have its ups and downs; "there is a time to weep and a time to laugh..." (Ecclesiastes 3:4). Even though we know tough times are coming our way, we are encouraged that it is only a season. If we get laid off from our jobs, if our children are being rebellious, if our friends turn their backs on us, or if we are being plagued by a pandemic, there will come a time when we get a new job, our children listen to us and thank us, we get friends who hold us through the difficult times, the pandemic ends and we can enjoy spending time with family and friends without worrying. The tough times won't last! Difficult seasons are a part of our journey in life, and in marriage we have a partner to help us navigate through the difficult seasons of life. But I am even more grateful that we can rely on God's strength to endure. And when we rely on God's strength, we get to know Him personally. We can say with confidence that God is a provider because He helped me put food on the table when I lost my job; God is a protector because he protected my children when they weren't listening to me; God is my friend because He held me when my friends turned their backs on me; God is a healer because He healed the world of a deadly virus. And because we get to know who God is on a personal level during the difficult seasons, we have the fortitude to praise Him during the calm seasons in life. We are encouraged because we can rejoice during the challenging times in life knowing that joy and strength are on the other side!

As I write this book, we are still in the middle of a pandemic where the COVID-19 virus is spreading rapidly around the world at alarming rates. It has been a challenging time for all of us as we have been living with this virus for almost two years now. What started as a few weeks of isolation turned into almost a year of not being able to see friends and family or go into the office to mingle with work colleagues. And even now that we can venture out of our homes, there are still restrictions. Some places require us to be vaccinated, other places require us to wear masks...life is just not the same as it was prior to the pandemic. Furthermore, many people have lost loved ones during the pandemic, and my husband and I are no exception.

My Uncle Paul had a long battle with lung cancer before it took his life at the start of the pandemic. He was at home alone because we were ordered to quarantine and it was days before someone found him. I had just given birth to Khaden Jr. about one month prior to his death, and my Uncle Paul did not have the chance to meet him. The next year, my husband's grandmother died unexpectedly in Trinidad before she had the chance to meet her great grandson. As I reflect on losing the people we loved dearly, it is a reminder for us to cherish the time we have with family and friends while they are here on this Earth; we must cherish the times to laugh. I believe this pandemic has taught us all that time with our loved ones is so precious and we must value the time we spend with them. Going through this painful season of the pandemic has taught us to be still and reflect on those things that truly matter in life. Therefore, I celebrate in knowing that this pandemic will be over, and I appreciate and value those who make this difficult season a little bit more manageable as we press through the weeping to get to the laughter.

Prayer:

Dear Heavenly Father,

Thank you for your love and strength, especially during the tough times. Give us the wisdom and discipline to rely on your strength to endure the difficult times. May we have the endurance to continue to press through the weeping in order to get to the laughter. Thank you for the challenging times, as they help us to know you better, and may we rejoice in every season because we know that you are with us.

In Jesus' name,

Amen.

Action:

I Do: Write about a time when you were going through a difficult time and it was resolved. This can serve as a reminder that when times are tough, it is only for a season.

_____

_____

_____

_____

We Do: Write about a time when your husband helped you to get through a difficult time in life. Now write a letter to thank him for being your support during this time, and tell him how much it meant to you.

Once you have completed the exercise with your husband, reflect on the following questions together:

Reflect on the current season of your life that you are in. Are you feeling encouraged? Discouraged?

_____

_____

_____

_____

How can you learn to be content with all seasons of life?

_____

_____

_____

_____

Scripture: John 14:27 (NIV)

"Peace I leave with you. My peace I give you. I do not give to you as the world gives. Do not let your hearts be troubled and do not be afraid."

Before Jesus is crucified, he has a discussion with disciples in order to prepare them for his leaving. In John 14:27, Jesus is preparing his disciples for when he leaves this Earth to return back to God. As Jesus talks with his disciples, he said he gives them peace. But this peace from Jesus is not a peace from the world. So what exactly is peace from Jesus? Peace from Jesus is a calming attitude in the midst of a storm, it is knowing that all will be ok because our true reward is in Heaven with God. We as Christians can have peace because Jesus has overcome the world! When Jesus died on the cross, He paid the price for our sins so that we can be in right relation with God. As a result, we will have eternal life. And we are encouraged because Jesus has overcome the world, we do not need to be afraid no matter what troubles we face in life.

When I was pregnant, my husband and I were practicing our spiritual exercise of memorizing scripture. Memorizing scripture is helpful in planting God's word in our heart so that we can live by God's word in our daily lives (Psalm 119:11). Each morning, my husband and I would say our memory verse out loud and sometimes we would recite the verse before we went to bed. This verse was especially helpful to my husband and I when we learned that our unborn son had a hole in his heart.

After my five month ultrasound, the doctor asked my husband and me to return for a follow-up appointment because the baby was not in a good position to view his heart. Because all of the ultrasounds and tests prior to the follow-up appointment had been successful and my husband and I were taking a lot of time off of work, I told my husband that he did not need to come to the follow-up appointment. When I went to the follow-up appointment, the doctor examined the ultrasound and told me that my son had a hole in his heart. My world felt like it was caving in, and I was in shock. The doctor then told me that she would refer me to a cardiac specialist so that I could get more information. She then reminded me that I still had time to terminate my pregnancy.

I was devastated. The thought of losing my active little baby boy who kicked me every day was overwhelming, but I held it together until I left the office, and then I wept. I immediately called my husband, who rushed to the doctor's office to see me and hold me and remind me that everything would be ok. My husband and I were both adamant about bringing our baby into the world because we had peace in knowing that everything would be ok; we had the peace of Jesus. But that does not mean that our journey was easy. Of course we worried for our son—we are human. There were many days and nights that I cried because I wanted my son to be ok. But even in the midst of worrying, we knew that everything would be alright. Because we had the peace of Jesus, we had the strength to fight for our baby boy. And when he was born, he had a successful heart surgery to repair the hole in his heart.

Prayer:

Dear Heavenly Father,

Thank you for giving us peace, especially in the midst of trying times. Your peace keeps us grounded, and we pray that we will have peace in all circumstances. May we focus on you so that our hearts won't be troubled and we won't be afraid. We love you Lord, and we thank you for the plans you have for our lives.

In Jesus' name,

Amen.

Action:

I Do: When was a time in your life when you needed God's peace? Did you get the peace you needed? Write down a Bible verse or verses that comforted you in that time.

_____

_____

_____

_____

We Do: As a couple, when was a time that you needed God's peace? How did you use God's peace to get through the trial?

_____

_____

_____

Once you have completed the exercise with your husband, reflect on the following questions together:

What kind of peace does knowing Jesus give?

_____

_____

_____

_____

How can this sense of peace encourage you in life? How can this sense of peace encourage you in your marriage?

_____

_____

_____

_____

Scripture: Romans 5:3-4 (NLT)

³ We can rejoice, too, when we run into problems and trials, for we know that they help us develop endurance. ⁴ And endurance develops strength of character, and character strengthens our confident hope of salvation.

How can we rejoice when we run into problems and trials? How can we rejoice when our husbands ignore us? How can we rejoice when our marriage seems like it is falling apart? How can we rejoice when our children don't listen to us? How can we rejoice when our bodies are sick and failing us? It is extremely hard to rejoice when we look at the physical aspects of the trials we face; the physical aspects of pain and fear can cause us to be disheartened when we face problems in our lives. However, we are encouraged to focus on the spiritual aspect when we endure trials. What does it mean to look at the spiritual aspect of a trial? It is looking beyond the physical and seeing how the fruits of the spirit are being produced or are growing through the trials that we face. Through this trial, are we learning how to love, be patient, have self-control (Galatians 5:23)? Are we learning how to rely on God for peace, joy, and faithfulness (Galatians 5:23)? When we take a pause to look at the spiritual aspect of the trials we face, we can rejoice because these trials help us to develop endurance that allows us to rely on God's strength and not our own. When we rely on God's omnipotent strength, we realize that our problems are extremely small in comparison, and we are able to face them with joy because God is on our side. In essence, each trial that we face and overcome increases our faith in God's strength, which helps us to overcome future trials that we endure. As we overcome our problems, we are better able to handle problems that come our way; we develop endurance.

The more problems we face, the more we learn to rely on God, which produces His character within us which are the fruits of the spirit: love, peace, joy, patience (Galatians 5:22). We rely on God so we become more patient; we rely on God so we become more loving; we rely on God so we become more kind. In essence, we are encouraged because the character that we produce is a reflection of God's character and it helps us to have a more solid Christian walk as we stand more solidly in God's Word and have hope in God's promises.

When my doctor told me that my son had a hole in his heart at my five-month check-up, I was distraught. I would go between periods of being ok and finding strength in my faith to other periods when I would break down crying and asking God, "Why me? Why must my son go through this?" I remember one time in particular when I called my parents in tears because I was wondering why God would allow my son to go through this trial of having a hole in his heart. As a mother, I felt helpless and guilty. *Was there something that I could have done to prevent this?* was a constant thought in my mind. But as I cried to my parents, my father boldly said, "Christina, you are looking at this from the physical. You need to look at this situation with spiritual eyes." And he kept repeating this throughout our conversation.

In the midst of my tears, I did not have the time or the mental capacity to process what he was saying to me, but after I hung up the phone and calmed down, I began to think more about what he really meant when he said I needed to look at my son's health issue through spiritual eyes. And as I thought about this statement, I remembered that it was 10 years ago when my mother told my sister, Amanda, and me that she had been diagnosed with breast cancer. When we received the news, we were devastated because cancer had taken my grandmother's and my cousin's lives, so we instantly thought the worst would happen. But with lots of prayer, chemotherapy, and radiation, my mother was in full remission and her cancer was gone. God had allowed my mother to be healed. And years prior to my mother telling me that she had breast cancer, my father collapsed at work and needed open heart surgery to repair his leaking heart valve. Our family was so grateful that he made a full recovery from his heart surgery, and now my unborn son would have to also have open heart surgery when he was born in order to repair the hole in his heart.

So when my father said that I needed to look at my trial through spiritual eyes, I believe he was reminding me that I have already seen God work miracles through the health of my parents. I believe my father wanted me to realize that God is bigger than the hole in my son's heart and that he is with me. My father wanted me to be confident in the omnipotence of the God that we serve. God had gotten me through some difficult trials with my parents' health and He could do it again with my son's health. My father wanted me to walk in the peace of knowing that God had everything under control. And as I began to look at my circumstance through spiritual eyes, I began to smile and be grateful. Thank you, Lord for seeing my parents through their health issues, and thank you for seeing me through my son's health issue. Through spiritual eyes, I was able to walk in faith, and be confident that God would carry me and my son throughout the process.

Prayer:

Dear Heavenly Father,

Thank you for the trials and problems that we face because they help us to rely on you. During these trials, we realize that you are bigger than anything we face, and that you will get us through it. We love you Lord, and we pray for increased faith and your peace during the hard times as you continue to give us the strength to endure.

In Jesus' name,

Amen.

Action:

I Do: Reflect on how a particular trial helped you to develop endurance or grow in the fruits of the Spirit (love, peace, joy, patience...). What can help you to rejoice during hard times? Is it thinking about how God has helped you in the past? Is it thinking about how God will help you get through? Is it repeating a Bible verse during the trial?

_____

_____

_____

_____

We Do: With your husband, reflect on how you both grew from a trial that you faced together and how it strengthened your faith.

Once you have completed the exercise with your husband, reflect on the following questions together:

Read Romans 5:3-4 together. Why can we rejoice when we run into trials? When we are facing hard times, what can we do to help us remember why we can rejoice during the hard times?

_____

_____

_____

[36] Be merciful, just as your Father is merciful. [37] Do not judge, and you will not be judged. Do not condemn, and you will not be condemned. Forgive, and you will be forgiven.

No one is perfect, including you and me. Jesus died on the cross to save us from our sins because we as imperfect humans were not capable of saving ourselves. In spite of our imperfection, God forgives us over and over and over and over again. There have been times when God spared us the punishment we deserved, and because of His mercy, we are to show mercy to others, especially our spouses. Showing mercy and forgiveness to each other is one way to keep the peace in our relationship and our household. So we are encouraged to not judge or condemn, but to be merciful and give forgiveness because God has been merciful to us.

When Khaden was courting me, we got into an argument, and I yelled and cursed at him. Yes, this sweet, saved Georgia peach stooped to a really low level, and it was very disrespectful. As soon as the words left my mouth, I immediately regretted them. When Khaden heard them, he calmly looked at me and said, "I respect you and I don't raise my voice at you, please give me that same respect." At that moment, I felt ashamed and saddened by my actions because Khaden was a great man and he did not deserve to be disrespected.

I immediately apologized, and my husband extended mercy to me and forgave me. Instead of yelling at me or returning my attitude, he was merciful and kind. Khaden didn't judge me or condemn me, and I was very humbled by his actions. Since that moment, I have been very careful to give my husband the respect he deserves, especially during the times we disagree. It is this type of attitude that brings healing and peace in our relationships.

Prayer:

Dear Heavenly Father,

Thank you for your mercy and your forgiveness. Thank you for not giving me the punishment I deserve. I pray that you help me to show mercy to my husband and that he shows mercy to me just as you have shown mercy to both of us. Help us to not judge or condemn one another, but to forgive as you have forgiven us. Thank you for your love and forgiveness.

In Jesus' name,

Amen.

Action:

I Do: Think about the times you have received mercy. I find that when you think about how much mercy you have received, it is easier to show others mercy.

We Do: Thank your husband for a time when he has shown you mercy and forgiven you.

Once you have completed the exercise with your husband, reflect on the following questions together:

Reflect on ways you can show each other mercy. What are some things that hinder you from giving mercy?

_____

_____

_____

_____

How can you overcome those things that hinder you from giving mercy?

_____

_____

_____

_____

_____

_____

Conclusion

Marriage is beautiful, but hard. The beauty in marriage is that we have a partner with us to experience the highs and lows that life may bring. The hard part in marriage is that we have a partner with us to experience the highs and lows that life may bring. Having a partner on our journey is beautiful because we can lean on them for support and comfort, but having a partner is also hard because we are both imperfect and we must work at learning how to continue to develop and deepen the bond of our marriages. As we grow in our marriage we learn more about our husbands and how to walk this life together, and as individuals we continue to evolve, grow, and change. It is important for us to evolve, grow, and change *with* our spouses— not *away* from them.

Marriage is hard, but beautiful. We go through challenges in life to help us grow, evolve, and change, and when we come out on the other side, we are stronger, knowing that God's strength is what got us through. That is the beauty of relying on God's strength to endure the hard times.

Love is choosing to value your spouse's needs above your own. It is an action and a heart change. So many times we get caught up in what our spouse does or how our spouse can change, but we should focus on what *we* do and how *we* can change. We have the power to control our actions and our mindset so that we can fully appreciate all that marriage has to offer. With hearts of gratitude and service, we can transform and rejuvenate our marriages to be full of love and purpose.

As we have seen in this book, God gives us the tools to experience life's highs and lows with our spouse and enjoy beauty in *all* of it. Thank you for visiting the **SPA**! I pray that you have been encouraged and will continue in the life-long fight for the beauty and rejuvenation of your marriage.

References

BibleProject. (2016, June 10). Overview: Ecclesiastes [Video]. YouTube. https://www.youtube.com/watch?v=lrsQ1tc-2wk

Collins. (n.d.). Spa. In Collinsditionary.com. Retrieved December 8, 2021, from https://www.collinsdictionary.com/us/dictionary/english/spa#:~:text=(sp%C9%91%20),order%20to%20improve%20their%20health.

Fay, B. (2021, May 13). Key Figures Behind America's Consumer Debt. Debt.org. Cleanup.https://www.debt.org/faqs/americans-in-debt/theoceancleanup.com/updates/whales-likely-impacted-by-great-pacific-garbage-patch/. Retrieved January 17, 2022.

Henry, Matthew. "Philippians 1." Bible Study Tools. 2019. https://www.biblestudytools.com/commentaries/matthew-henry-concise/philippians/1.html. Retrieved June 12, 2019.

Palmer, S. & Palmer, B. (2012). *The Five Money Personalities: Speaking the Same Love and Money Languages*. Thomas Nelson.

Smith, L. (2018, Jan 7). Dr. Phil Opens Up About His 2 Keys To a Happy Marriage And The Question Couples Should Ask Daily. *Lifestyle*. https://littlethings.com/lifestyle/dr-phil-marriage-tips

Strong, J. (1890). *Strong's exhaustive concordance of the Bible*. Abingdon Press.

www.ingramcontent.com/pod-product-compliance
Lightning Source LLC
LaVergne TN
LVHW051249080426
835513LV00016B/1829